Kay Nielsen

Kay Nielsen

Introduction by Keith Nicholson

CORONET BOOKS
Hodder and Stoughton

KAY NIELSEN

Copyright © 1975 by Bantam Books, Inc.
All rights reserved under International and
Pan-American Conventions

This edition published 1975 by Coronet Books

Printed in Italy by Arnoldo Mondadori Editore,
for Coronet Books,
Hodder and Stoughton,
St. Paul's House,
Warwick Lane,
London EC4P 4AH.

Published simultaneously in the United States and Canada

ISBN 0 340 18983 5

'All this I have seen in the dreams of the night clearer than I can force myself to see in dreams of the day.'

WILLIAM MORRIS: A DREAM OF JOHN BALL

Nostalgia for a Golden Age, it would seem, is part of the human condition. In times of great social upheaval and stress men look to the past for solace or escape from present evils. L.P. Hartley likened the past to a foreign country, and history, indeed, is like a map where we can retrace our steps and find new routes to an ideal destination. Not only objective time past but our own memorable childhood offers a territorial perspective for the rediscovery of lost innocence and joys. Hence the potency of myth, legend and fairy-tale, peopled by the exotic and the bizarre, where man's predicament is effectively symbolized. Such a world was inhabited by the Danish artist and designer Kay Nielsen. What Nielsen offers in his beautiful paintings and book illustrations is not merely an escape from the mindlessness of modern existence. His retreat into a world of childhood fantasy is no innocent indulgence; it is where, like his romantic predecessors, he finds the imagination can conceive of infinite possibility and grasp an alternative vision where hope remains undimmed.

Visionaries of the 19th Century, like William Morris, Walt Whitman, Carlyle and Ruskin, appalled by the horrors and ravages of industrialism, pointed the way from a blind mechanical 'progress' to a simpler, more meaningful life. The Pre-Raphaelite Brotherhood and the Aesthetic Movement did not represent a narrow Victorian art-for-art's-sake philosophy as is often alleged. Their artistic manifesto, whether based upon models from the Middle Ages or early Renaissance, expressed an all-pervasive yearning for a beauteous vision. The printed book was the means by which this visionary 'propaganda' was disseminated. By the 1890s, largely due to the influence of these 'movements' and men like Morris and his Kelmscott Press, the book had become an object of great beauty as well as knowledge. By a happy coincidence, the perfection of new techniques in printing enabled publishers, at modest cost, to produce books of astonishing quality, the like of which we shall never see again. At this time the English were out to civilize the world and their language had become the lingua franca of civilization. London was the throbbing heart of a mighty empire upon which the sun never set. To this magnet was attracted the artistic and literary talent the world had to offer. While the English were in Africa, India and the Far East, the world came to England, to admire and to learn. Writers and painters from America and Europe were to settle in London and make it their home. Many new publishing houses, mostly of German origin, came into being (and thrive to this day). Artists from France (Edmund Dulac), Belgium (Jean de Bosschère) and America (Frank Cheyne Papé) arrived to complement the army of indigenous book illustrators already at work (among them Arthur Rackham, Hugh Thomson, the Robinsons and the Brothers Brock). How curious that so much talent—not to mention genius—should be available at the most opportune time (as in the case of Hollywood some two or three decades later).

A relatively late arrival was the young Dane, Kay Rasmus Nielsen, fresh from his studies in Paris and anxious to arrange an exhibition of his work. Nielsen was born in Copenhagen in 1886 of most distinguished parents. His mother was the celebrated actress Oda Larssen, and his father, Professor Martinius Nielsen, also a classical actor in his younger days, became Director of the Royal Danish Theater. Youthful recollections of the artist included Ibsen, Björnson, Grieg and Lie, visitors to the Nielsen household. The young boy would illustrate the traditional folklore and sagas of the Norsemen as they were read aloud by his mother. From the age of 12 he was tutored privately, but in

1904, after considering a medical career, he left for Paris to pursue his great passion for art in the schools of Montparnasse. He studied at the Académie Julienne under J.P. Laurens and subsequently at Calerossi's. It was at this time, like so many other young artists, that Nielsen became fascinated by the work of Aubrey Beardsley. As a boy Nielsen had been visually excited by the drawings his grandfather had brought back from the Far East. Beardsley was the artist par excellence who had absorbed these influences and evolved them into his own inimitable style. It was the Japanese woodcuts of Hokusai, Hiroshige and Utamaro that had such an effect upon Western art when they reached Paris in the later 19th Century. The simplified and formalized landscapes of the Japanese represented an exciting and unfamiliar perspective that was to be assimilated by artists in Vienna, Moscow (in the work of Bilibin) and New York, as well as Paris. The asymmetry of their compositions, the frequent diagonal stress, the vacant white space surrounding the figures and the high viewpoint were characteristic of these cultured, two-dimensional woodcuts. Perhaps of all the constituents that came together to form what we understand as Art Nouveau the contribution of the Japanese was the most significant. And as an exponent of this style it was Beardsley perhaps who

deserved the most praise and earned the most notoriety. In England his startling graphic work in black and white offered an extraordinary challenge to the historicism of Morris and Burne-Jones, his early masters. It was the fastidiousness, the ostentation, but more particularly the unwholesome excess of the later Beardsley which most captured the imagination of the impulsive and pessimistic young Nielsen.

THE EXHIBITIONS

The Book of Death, a series of black and white drawings after Beardsley, were the principal illustrations Kay Nielsen chose to put before the public at his first exhibition after his arrival in London in 1911. These were shown at the Dowdeswell Galleries in New Bond Street in July the following year. (As these illustrations were never issued in book form—a fate which befell much of Nielsen's work—the only copies which survive are those printed with contemporary reviews of the exhibition. The originals are in private collections or have been lost.) *The Book of Death* series represented a high sense of drama in Nielsen's outlook and the exhibition was a great success. The theme—the love of Pierrot for a beautiful young maiden—as well as the sincerity of the artist's mood, largely accounted for their popularity. A sharp foreboding—some presage of imminent disaster—is ever present to the lovers. The first drawing, entitled *Omen*. the third, *Inevitable*, and the fifth, called *The Chasm*. perhaps sufficiently explain the story. Pierrot is separated from his innamorata by death, and in his despair seeks destruction in the deep dark tomb of the beloved. *The Chasm*. in fact, shows the desperate lover flinging roses into the sepulcher as he prepares to take the fatal plunge into the darkness below. In *The Vision* and *Yearning* we see Pierrot struggling to regain the beloved one—not now in her mere bodily beauty and effulgent youth, but in the finer essence of the spirit. *The End*. the last of the series, is inevitable. In contrast to the Strindbergian morbidity of the collection, the mood of which keenly anticipates impending world events, and some equally lugubrious settings of poems by Heine, Nielsen also included designs for water colors of *Hans Andersen* and the collection *In Powder and Crinoline:* that were published later.

With the publication of *In Powder and Crinoline* in 1913, Nielsen held an exhibition of the original water colors at the Leicester Galleries in November of that year. It is ironic that artists received very little payment for their work from publishers and depended almost entirely upon sales of their original work at private exhibitions to make a living.

(Beardsley was paid what was considered a handsome fee—in 1893—for his Morte d'Arthur illustrations but these occupied him for 18 months.) With these water colors Nielsen had entered the second phase of his career, emancipated from the Beardsley tradition and indebted to the great Chinese colorists for inspiration. While the art of all young painters is bound to be derivative, Nielsen shows in his development a fancy so delicate and an outlook so original that no charge of plagiarism can be brought against him. His color work is delicate and suggestive rather than forceful. Very lovely in its faint blues and greens with tones of peach is the illustration Plate 21 where the high folly, the love birds and the blossom testify to the legacy of Japan. Properly subdued to the scheme of a purely decorative theme is the illustration to the story of *Rosanie* Plate 25; yet here again and in Plates 26 and 29 the Beardsley tradition is evident. Inimitable as a study of character is the glimpse of the early Victorian coulisse in *The Man Who Never Laughed* where Nielsen has struck a pretty vein of his own. The louche, blear-eyed waiter fingering his money is a study in himself. Another illustration to this story, Plate 27, has all the grimness of Edvard Munch, and both this and the curious mixture of black and color in Plate 28 represent Nielsen at his most menacing and grotesque.

East of the Sun and West of the Moon was published in 1914 and the exhibition of water colors took place in March the following year. These 25 illustrations represent Nielsen at his most celebrated and certainly at his most spectacular. An advance in strength and decorative feeling on his former illustrations is very marked. The great charm of these paintings lies in the artist's power of combining eerie suggestion with beautiful decorative effect. The drawings are immediately understandable and clearly convey the details of the scenes they are intended to depict so that a child can follow the incidents of a story-book in them. At the same time each drawing is conceived as a decorative composition, admirably balanced and spaced and with the masses of black, white or color arranged in harmonic unison. Among the most successful is Plate 10, where Nielsen's predilection for height, flow and decorative effect is noticeable. Whatever style he adopts, and this is very much determined by subject matter, his individuality is sufficiently strong to make it his own. A flavor of art nouveau is especially noticeable in the modernity of Plate 5, and in the elaborate curves of his foam-topped waves in some other drawings, but this is a diminishing influence. Above all this collection has the authenticity of felt experience—the scent of the pine forest, the ice of the polar flows, the solitary birch in the arctic waste, the creatures that inhabit the lands of fjord and midnight sun, the heroes of Lied and Saga.

Nielsen staged an exhibition of his works in New York in 1917 and then returned to Copenhagen as the war ended. This period of his life is marked by his close friendship and collaboration with the young actor and producer Johannes Poulsen, a pioneer of Danish cinema, with whom he shared great similarities of artistic feeling. In 1919 they mounted a spectacular production of *Aladdin* in the poetic version by Adam Oehlenschlaeger at the Danish State Theater, the performance extending over two evenings. Nielsen designed the sets and costumes, recreating on a Northern stage the glories and wonders of the East, with its wealth of light and color, of shadows dark and somber (an undertaking that must have been very close to his heart). From contemporary accounts we understand that he succeeded in evolving from his lurid imagination scenes of the most fantastic beauty and splendor. In 1922 Nielsen and Poulsen mounted a similar epic production of *Scaramouche* for which Nielsen also made drawings for the published score of the music by Sibelius. Later productions included *The Poet's Dream* and Ostrovsky's *The Storm*.

Nielsen returned to London for the publication of his edition of *Hans Andersen* in 1924 and the exhibition was held in February. The collection also included set designs for *Aladdin* and *Scaramouche* as well as a series of illustrations for *The Arabian Nights* and *The Rubáiyát of Omar Khayyám* (alas never published). The paintings for *Hans Andersen* are difficult to assess as some of them date from an earlier period and his work in black and white, particularly *The Shepherdess and the Chimney Sweeper.* Influences of the East, in *The Nightingale,* and a rare acknowledgement to Edmund Dulac, in *The Hardy Tin Soldier,* are apparent.

Nielsen married, in 1926, twenty-two-year-old Ulla Pless-Schmidt, and in December 1930 was back in London for his last exhibition at Leicester Square, where the *Red Magic* drawings and the illustrations for *The Brothers Grimm* were on sale. This collection, which also included a set of drawings for Heine's *The Old Old Story.* is somewhat disappointing. It is sad to notice a considerable diminution of the artist's powers. Although it is clear Nielsen was attempting an approach akin to folk-art for these settings, the angular austerity of the designs, the absence of decoration and his usual obsessive detail, and particularly the thinness of color, suggest a decline in inspiration.

In 1936 Nielsen traveled to Hollywood with Poulsen to mount a production of *Jedermann* (based upon the early English *Everyman*) by Hugo von Hofmannsthal. Poulsen died soon after in 1938 and Nielsen settled in Los Angeles, where he worked in the wilderness that was then Hollywood, as an actor, director, set designer and muralist until his death in obscurity in 1957.

THE PUBLISHED WORKS

1913 *In Powder and Crinoline:* Old Fairy Tales retold by Sir Arthur Quiller-Couch: 24 colored plates by Nielsen including an oval frontispiece. Published by Hodder & Stoughton in an edition limited to 500 copies, numbered and signed by the Artist. Folio format, bound in heavy green vellum decorated in gilt with silk ties. A most sumptuous production much sought after by collectors. Printed by Henry Stone of Banbury with title inventions and ornate borders. A trade edition in cloth, equally scarce, was also produced.

1914 *East of the Sun and West of the Moon:* Old Tales from the North (15 Selections from the Norske Folkeeventyr of Asbjörnsen and Moe): 25 colored plates by Nielsen. Published by Hodder & Stoughton in an edition limited to 500 copies, numbered and signed by the Artist (a publisher's blurb mentions only 250 copies of the De Luxe Edition, priced at two guineas!). Folio format bound in white vellum decorated in gilt. Another superb production, with tipped-in plates, gilt head, vignette title and black and gilt pictorial end-papers by Nielsen. A trade edition in blue cloth is more likely to be encountered but both editions are very scarce.

1924 *Hans Andersen's Fairy Tales:* (16 Stories): 12 mounted colored plates by Nielsen: Edition De Luxe in white vellum limited to 500 copies, numbered and signed by the Artist. Folio format published by Hodder & Stoughton. A trade edition in cloth also exists. (Hodder & Stoughton published another edition of Hans Andersen in 1913, illustrated by Heath Robinson, which probably explains the late appearance of the Nielsen edition, a set of drawings for which existed in 1912.)

1925 *Hansel and Gretel:* Stories from the Brothers Grimm: 12 colored plates by Nielsen are tipped-in. Published by Hodder & Stoughton in a De Luxe Edition limited to 600 copies, numbered and signed by the Artist. Folio format bound in white silken linen decorated in blue and gilt. Title in red and black and the end-papers are decorated in a red and gilt floral design by Nielsen. The plates were printed by Henry Stone and the text by Constable in

Edinburgh. There is a trade edition and an edition in French published the same year in illustrated paper-wrappers. This latter, under the title *Fleur-de-Neige* (Snow White), was published by L'Édition d'Art in Paris in an edition limited to 2400 copies, 400 of which were on vellum.

1930 *Red Magic:* A Collection of the World's Best Fairy Tales from all Countries: Edited and Arranged by Romer Wilson: With 8 colored plates and 50 black and white textual illustrations by Nielsen. Published by Jonathan Cape in red cloth with a gilt title in a trade edition only. Octavo format, the plates were unmounted and the edition as a whole was rather inauspicious.

Kay Nielsen has passed into history. He belonged to a Golden Age of books and illustrations. But when we see his work—time-locked and enduring—we too can share his vision and dream of more wonderful things.

'Was it a vision, or a waking dream?
Fled is that music:—Do I wake or sleep?'
JOHN KEATS

Keith Nicholson

1) "Well, mind and hold tight by my shaggy coat, and then
    there's nothing to fear," said the Bear, so she rode a
    long, long way

East of the Sun and West of the Moon
East of the Sun West of the Moon

HODDER & STOUGHTON

2) "Tell me the way, then," she said, "and I'll search you out"

East of the Sun and West of the Moon
East of the Sun West of the Moon

HODDER & STOUGHTON

3) And then she lay on a little green patch in the midst
of the gloomy thick wood

East of the Sun and West of the Moon
East of the Sun West of the Moon

HODDER & STOUGHTON

4) No sooner had he whistled than he heard a whizzing and a
       whirring from all quarters, and such a large flock of
    birds swept down that they blackened all the field in which
                        they settled

           The Three Princesses in the Blue Mountain
              East of the Sun West of the Moon

HODDER & STOUGHTON

5) The Lad in the Bear's skin, and the King of Arabia's
daughter

The Blue Belt

East of the Sun West of the Moon

HODDER & STOUGHTON

6) She saw the Lindworm for the first time, as he came in
and stood by her side

Prince Lindworm

East of the Sun West of the Moon

HODDER & STOUGHTON

7) She could not help setting the door a little ajar, just
to peep in, when—Pop! out flew the Moon

The Lassie and Her Godmother
East of the Sun West of the Moon

HODDER & STOUGHTON

8) Then he coaxed her down and took her home

The Lassie and her Godmother
East of the Sun West of the Moon

HODDER & STOUGHTON

9) "Here are your children; now you shall have them again.
   I am the Virgin Mary"

The Lassie and Her Godmother
East of the Sun West of the Moon

HODDER & STOUGHTON

10) He too saw the image in the water; but he looked up at once,
and became aware of the lovely lassie who sate there up in
the tree

The Lassie and Her Godmother
East of the Sun West of the Moon

HODDER & STOUGHTON

11) "You'll come to three Princesses, whom you will see standing in the earth up to their necks, with only their heads out"

The Three Princesses of Whiteland
East of the Sun West of the Moon

HODDER & STOUGHTON

12) So the man gave him a pair of snow shoes

The Three Princesses of Whiteland
East of the Sun West of the Moon

HODDER & STOUGHTON

13) The six brothers riding out to woo

The Giant Who Had No Heart In His Body
East of the Sun West of the Moon

HODDER & STOUGHTON

14) "On that island stands a church; in that church is a well; in that well swims a duck"

The Giant Who Had No Heart In His Body
East of the Sun West of the Moon

HODDER & STOUGHTON

15) When he had walked for a day or so, a strange man met him.
"Whither away?" asked the man

The Widow's Son
East of the Sun West of the Moon

HODDER & STOUGHTON

16) But still the Horse begged him to look behind him

The Widow's Son
East of the Sun West of the Moon

HODDER & STOUGHTON

17) And this time she whisked off the wig; and there lay the
lad, so lovely, and white and red, just as the Princess
had seen him in the morning sun

The Widow's Son
East of the Sun West of the Moon

HODDER & STOUGHTON

18) Just as they bent down to take the rose a big dense snowdrift
came and carried them away

The Three Princesses in the Blue Mountain
East of the Sun West of the Moon

HODDER & STOUGHTON

19) As soon as they tugged at the rope, the Captain and the
Lieutenant pulled up the Princesses, the one after the
other

The Three Princesses in the Blue Mountain
East of the Sun West of the Moon

HODDER & STOUGHTON

20) And there on a thone all covered with black sat
the Iron King

Minon-Minette
In Powder and Crinoline

HODDER & STOUGHTON

21) List, ah, list to the zephyr in the grove!
    Where beneath the happy boughs
    Flora builds her summerhouse:
Whist! ah, whist! while the cushat tells his love.

Felicia or The Pot of Pinks
In Powder and Crinoline

HODDER & STOUGHTON

22) Felicia thereupon stepped forth, and terrified though
she was, saluted the Queen respectfully: with so
graceful a curtsey

Felicia or The Pot of Pinks
In Powder and Crinoline

HODDER & STOUGHTON

24) The Princesses on the way to the dance

The Twelve Dancing Princesses
In Powder and Crinoline

HODDER & STOUGHTON

25) "I have had such a terrible dream," she declared.
"... a pretty bird swooped down, snatched it from
my hands and flew away with it"

Rosanie or The Inconstant Prince
In Powder and Crinoline

HODDER & STOUGHTON

26) A look—a kiss—and he was gone

Rosanie or The Inconstant Prince
In Powder and Crinoline

HODDER & STOUGHTON

27) And the mirror told him that his were indeed the
withered face and form

The Man Who Never Laughed
In Powder and Crinoline

HODDER & STOUGHTON

28) "Your soul!—My soul!" they kept saying in
hollow tones, according as they won or lost

John and the Ghosts
In Powder and Crinoline

HODDER & STOUGHTON

29) "Don't drink!" cried out the little Princess, springing
to her feet; "I would rather marry a gardener!"

The Twelve Dancing Princesses
In Powder and Crinoline

HODDER & STOUGHTON

30) And they built a crystal coffin

Snow White—Fleur-de-Neige

Fleur-de-Neige et D'autres Contes de Grimm

L'ÉDITION D'ART

31) The Cottage was built of bread and cake

Hansel and Gretel—Hansel et Gretel

Fleur-de-Neige et D'autres Contes de Grimm

L'EDITION D'ART

32) He recognised the fair Cerise
Cerise, or the Married Frog—Cerise ou la Grenouille Mariée
Fleur-de-Neige et D'autres Contes de Grimm

L'EDITION D'ART

33) His wife was seated on a golden throne

The Fisherman and his wife—Le Pêcheur et sa Femme
Fleur-de-Neige et D'autres Contes de Grimm

L'EDITION D'ART

34)   The Prince knelt down and gave her a kiss
Sleeping Beauty—Rose D'Épine
Fleur-de-Neige et D'autres Contes de Grimm
L'EDITION D'ART

35) Blow, blow light winds!

The Goosegirl—La Gardeuse D'Oies

Fleur-de-Neige et D'autres Contes de Grimm

L'EDITION D'ART

36) The King could not find her
Noir-de-Fumée
Fleur-de-Neige et D'autres Contes de Grimm
L'EDITION D'ART

37) He struck the ground angrily with his right foot

Saute-Menu

Fleur-de-Neige et D'autres Contes de Grimm

L'EDITION D'ART

38) The Unicorn drove her horn into the tree

The Brave Little Tailor—Le Vaillant Petit Tailleur

Fleur-de-Neige et D'autres Contes de Grimm

L'EDITION D'ART

39) Six white swans were flying high in the sky

The White Swans—Les Cynes Blancs
Fleur-de-Neige et D'autres Contes de Grimm

L'EDITION D'ART

40) Out of the fire jumped a little bird

The Juniper Tree—Le Genévrier
Fleur-de-Neige et D'autres Contes de Grimm

L'EDITION D'ART